HOW TO INCREASE YOUR WEALTH

Ultimate Guide To Budget Your Money

CONTENTS

LET'S START

There are two kinds of people in this world: those who say they are going to do something and those who actually do it. I want you to understand that once you open this book, you should aspire to be a person who takes action rather than just talking about it. First, you have to genuinely want to accomplish what needs to be done, and it's not enough to merely tell yourself that you want to save money. Anyone can utter words, and while words hold power, without corresponding actions, they carry little meaning.

Now that we've identified the two types of people, which one are you going to choose? Now that we've let go of all the people who aren't serious, let's dive into how to save and grow your money. If you're not interested in growing your money, we'll explore how to reduce that lingering debt that weighs on your mind. You know what I'm talking about, right?

Remember, the first step is genuinely wanting to do it. The first thing you need to do is take a look at that credit card. You know, the one in your purse, wallet, or even on your dresser. Take a good look at it, and then cut it up. Yes, you read that correctly. The number one thing you need to do is put a stop to temptation. While you may think it's harmless to keep your credit card around, deep down, it encourages you to keep spending, even if it's only on credit. You have to eliminate the temptation, but I won't sugarcoat it; it's not as easy as you might think. We're not here because it's easy; nothing in life is easy, but it does get easier with time.

<u>Now, let me ask you, what is your highest bill, or what's the largest loan you owe? How long have you been carrying this amount of debt?</u>

____

____

____

____

____

____

____

____

Do you see how that looks now? Whether it has been a long or short period, the fact remains that you still have unpaid debt. Moreover, you haven't been saving as you should because you can't seem to control your spending, is that correct? Don't worry; you're not alone in this struggle. In fact, I faced the same issues until I devised a plan that actually worked for me. This plan may also work for you, or you might need to make some adjustments, but it's effective nonetheless.

I want you to be aware that "The average American debt totals $59,580, including mortgages, auto loans, student loans, and credit card debt," as reported by Business Insider. This debt can be attributed to various factors, including inflation, but it doesn't mean your debt has to remain that high or close to it. There are many tools available to help you reduce your debt, and I'm going to provide them to you and show you how they can benefit you in the long run.

TIME TO SAVE

Everybody wants to save but doesn't know how; I can admit I was like that once upon a time. Saving isn't easy, especially in this economy, but there are still things you can do. It's not a helpless situation; it just takes time, patience, self-discipline, and a focus on the future rather than the present. You have to stop giving in to impulsive purchases. This applies to both big and small expenses because every purchase matters. Even if you think that small expenses like dining out, buying snacks, or non-essential items don't make a significant impact, you're wrong. Every expenditure counts, and in fact, I would argue that smaller ones matter even more than larger ones because small expenses gradually add up to significant sums.

For instance, if you visit the store five days a week and spend $10 each day, that's $50 spent. Instead of saving or paying off some bills, you've spent that money. Now, if you had chosen to eat at home rather than eating out, you would be $50 richer. It may not seem like much, but consider how much you spend in a month using this logic – that's $200 spent on eating out. I'm not suggesting that you should never eat out, but it's a considerable amount of money to be spending on food. Small expenses add up, so take a moment to think about what you could do with that extra money in your pocket. This is one of the cornerstones of saving; you need to assess how much everything costs you, even small purchases, and see if there's a way to reduce your spending on outside food. This may vary from person to person, but the fact remains that unnecessary spending on food is happening.

As my mother and many other parents would say, "There's food at home." For some, breaking this habit might be easy, but for others, it can be challenging because, like all habits, it's difficult to break once it's established. According to the University of Cincinnati in America, this year alone, there has been a 20% increase in eating out at restaurants and opting for outside food instead of cooking at home. Are you part of that 20%? If you are, you know where to start in order to change your habits and save your money.

These are just the basics of saving money because everyone enjoys food. If you can change your food-eating habits, you can change other habits too. If you find it challenging, just imagine having extra cash in your pocket that could be directed towards savings or investments that could increase your net worth. Isn't it a great feeling to know you're taking steps to have more? Remember, everything starts with a mindset.

The second most important aspect that often gets overlooked when it comes to saving money is your weekly activities. Yes, this is different from dining out. I'm referring to going out to clubs, partying, bowling, or engaging in any activities that cost money but aren't necessities. In today's world, everything seems to come with a hefty price tag, and I understand the desire to have fun. Instead of indulging in such costly activities, why not have a game night with friends using games you already own or that a friend has? You can still have a great time while spending less and saving more.

Many people find this challenging, but it really isn't if you're committed to making positive changes in your life. If you're not ready to act, then you shouldn't be picking up a book about savings. I remember a time when I used to go out every weekend, party, and attend various activities, but by the end of the weekend, I was left broke. I was living paycheck to paycheck, and the cycle repeated itself week after week. Let me tell you, that's no way to live, especially if you want to get ahead financially, save for a rainy day, or buy your own house.

While I've been primarily discussing saving, it's important to note that investing is also a way to save, as it can make your money grow. That's something I aimed for, and I encourage you to do the same. Most people won't share the secrets of saving, but I'll tell you that the key is the desire to do it and putting in the effort to cut down on spending as much as possible. This way, you won't find yourself living paycheck to paycheck or relying on others for money until your next payday because you were irresponsible with your finances. I understand that these two things aren't the easiest to accomplish, but I urge you to practice them so that you can start seeing more of your money and stop wondering where it all went.

<u>Now, let me ask you, how much money would you estimate you spend on outside activities and dining out? And how do you plan to reduce your spending in these areas?</u>

____

____

____

____

____

____

____

Even though cutting back on going out most weekends or during the week can save you a significant amount of money, if you aren't able to do that just yet, remember that most things require baby steps. You can start by seeking discounts on the activities you enjoy while still saving money and having fun. Many people overlook the benefits of discounts and rewards offered to members for certain things.

Always make it a habit to search for discounts before going out or booking anything; you'll be surprised at what you can find. This can also help you shift your mindset towards saving money. Don't hesitate to look for coupons as well. I know it may sound unconventional in 2023, but they are still out there; you just need to hunt for them, and it shouldn't be as challenging as you might think.

GOOD DEBT

You're probably looking at the title of this chapter and wondering why we're discussing "debt" when it doesn't seem related to saving money. Well, I'll answer that question shortly, but it's always good to start with the positive before delving into the negative. Good debt is one of those positive aspects you need to be aware of, and it should be considered a crucial life skill. Unfortunately, schools often overlook this topic, at least where I'm from. So, let me take a moment to educate you, so you can, in turn, educate others.

In simple terms, good debt is debt that brings you financial benefits. If that concept isn't clear to you, let me break it down further because sometimes it's not immediately obvious. One example of good debt is taking out a loan for a business. However, I don't want to confuse you; you should only consider this if you have a well-thought-out business plan with expected profits and more. Don't rush into a business loan just because it has the word "good" attached to it. That could backfire, which is why another rule is to do thorough research before taking out a loan, especially for business ventures. According to Forbes, only about half of small businesses survive past the first five years of operation. This doesn't mean I'm discouraging you from starting a business. Like the rest of this book, I'm here to show you how to save and be cautious about your spending.

Another example of good debt is taking out a loan to purchase a property. Before you ask, I mean a property to rent out. You can live in it, but renting it out to tenants can generate additional income. This approach allows you to increase your net worth while your tenants help pay off your loans. You'll be able to meet your monthly loan payments and even make a profit. Just like most things in life, this isn't an easy process, and you should only explore it if you've done some research or have experience in the real estate field. If you lack experience, consider finding a mentor to guide you.

If you're still not entirely clear on what constitutes good debt, here's one more example. I want you to fully grasp that, despite the negative connotations often associated with debt, there is such a thing as good debt. Student loans fall into this category. I know what you might be thinking, so hear me out. Student loans are taken out to invest in education, which can lead to higher-paying jobs. Consider this perspective: there are different types of students and levels of education, but I'm specifically talking about taking out a loan for professions such as becoming a doctor or lawyer. Yes, I acknowledge it's a common saying, but think about it. Jobs like being a doctor or lawyer are likely to be in demand consistently, especially doctors. Legal issues are always arising, so if you dedicate years to becoming a lawyer and manage your career effectively, you can pay off those loans.

I'll keep emphasizing this until it sinks in: there's always a risk associated with taking out any kind of loan. I'm merely informing you about the good kinds of loans that are more likely to bring returns and increase your net worth. Many degrees can achieve that, regardless of your field of study. Don't let anything discourage you from pursuing your passions, as long as you understand the risks of taking out a loan, whether it's for education or any other aspect of life. The goal is to grow your wealth, not accumulate more debt. Even though some investments take longer than others, in the end, you're still enhancing your financial well-being through good debt.

GOOD DEBT

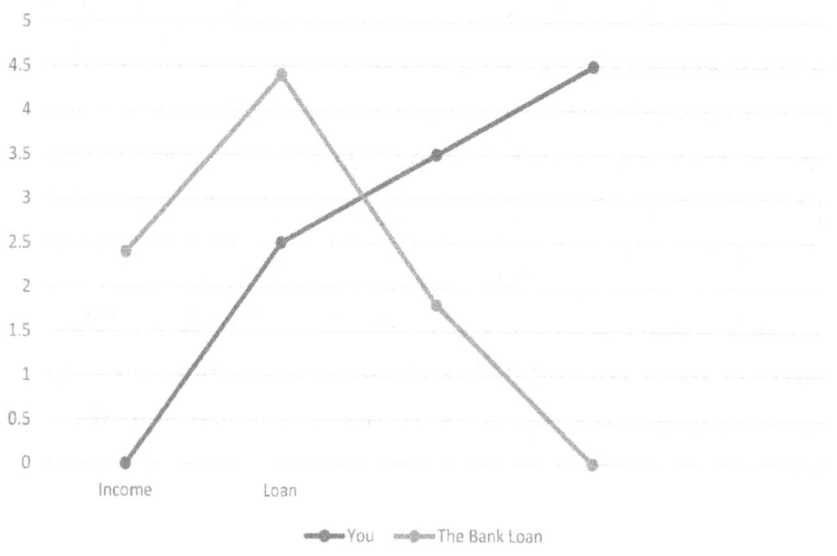

This is an example of how good debt can work effectively over the course of several years when used correctly. In this example, you can observe how, as the years progress, your wealth increases while the loan decreases. This ultimately results in you earning significantly more money over a five-year period. The chart above illustrates the growth of the loan, primarily due to interest accruing over time. The longer you have a loan outstanding, the more it increases solely due to interest. But don't worry; we'll delve into that topic later.

For now, it's crucial to grasp how good debt operates and how it can benefit you.

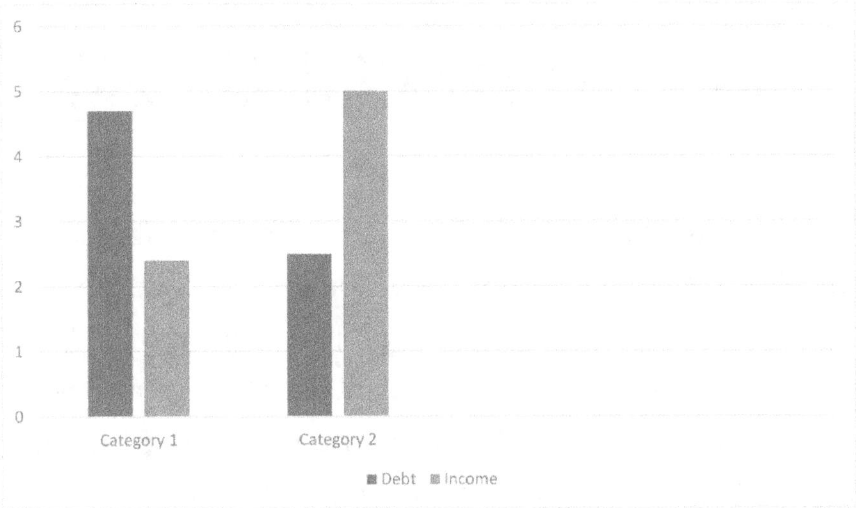

Here's another example of how your debt can impact you if it isn't the beneficial kind. In the first section, you can observe that over the course of a few years, your debt exceeds your income. This is a situation you want to steer clear of because getting out of debt can be incredibly challenging, especially if your income doesn't match your expectations. But don't worry; that's precisely why you're here, and we're committed to helping you climb out of that financial hole you might have accidentally fallen into.

Now, in the second section, you can see that your income surpasses the loan you took out. This is the ultimate goal — to have that beneficial debt where you borrowed money, but in the end, it generates significantly more income than you initially borrowed.

CAN'T GET ENOUGH SAVINGS

Everyone understands the concept of "saving," but many people fail to put it into practice. Some may argue that you need to work harder to save or live a good life, but I personally believe that no one should need more than one job to achieve savings and live comfortably. One of the most underestimated methods of saving, which many people overlook, is living below your means. If you can manage to do this, you're already ahead of most people.

The human mind can sometimes play tricks on you, and one of the primary tricks is believing that if you earn more, you can spend more. However, even with higher earnings, you may still not be saving enough or retaining sufficient money. Life is about living comfortably without struggling from paycheck to paycheck.

Another effective way to save money is to stop online shopping! In today's world, it's incredibly easy to purchase things with just a click of a button. However, this convenience can be detrimental to your financial restraint. One approach that has worked for me is deleting shopping apps from your phone or unlinking your credit and debit cards from online stores. This extra step might make you think twice before making impulse purchases.

You can train your mind to reconsider whether you truly need that new air fryer, which is slightly bigger than the one you already own, or a new rice pot when your current one works perfectly fine. Before clicking "checkout" on websites like Shein, Amazon, or Walmart, ask yourself if you genuinely need the item or if you simply want it because it's new. If it takes you more than a few seconds to decide, chances are you don't actually need it. If it's not a necessity, refrain from making the purchase, and keep that money in your pocket for something you genuinely require. This process may take months to master, but remember, Rome wasn't built in a day. Every dollar you save is a dollar you keep in your pocket, rather than giving it to a corporation.

There are many ways to save that people often overlook, such as reviewing and potentially changing your cell phone plan. In 2023, most places have Wi-Fi available in their buildings and homes. So, do you really need an unlimited 5G plan when you have Wi-Fi everywhere you go? Likely not. Contact your phone provider and explore options for a more cost-effective plan that uses fewer data GB.

Now, let's do some math together. If your phone plan, on your own, costs $100 per month, multiplying that by 12 months means you're spending roughly $1,200 per year on your phone bill alone. However, if you can reduce it to $80 per month, that's only $900 per year, which means you've saved around $300 annually on your phone bill alone. Doesn't that sound like a great way to save money? I can't stress enough that it's the little things that you may not think matter or add up, but they often make a significant difference.

While we're on this subject, let's consider your cable and home Wi-Fi. Are they billed separately, or do you have them as a package deal? It makes a difference. Depending on your service provider, there may be discounts available when you bundle them together instead of paying for them separately. In some cases, having them separately might be more cost-effective, so do your research and determine which option saves you more money.

This book is all about preserving your hard-earned money, even if it's just a few dollars at a time. Those small savings add up over the course of a year. Take a step back and calculate how much you spend annually on extra activities, food, cell phone plans, and Wi-Fi – you might be surprised at how much you can save by making informed choices.

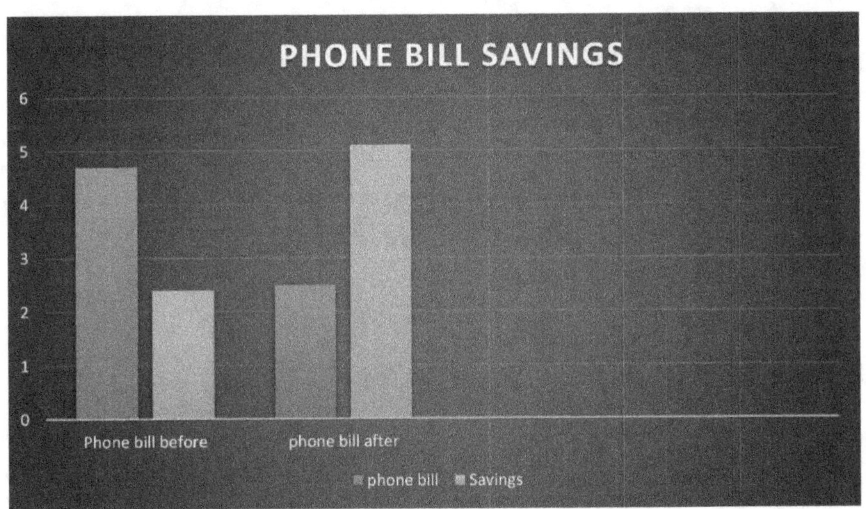

In this example, you can observe that by reducing your phone bill, you can save more money and retain it in your pocket. This is the essence of it all. So, before your next billing cycle, strive to find ways to keep more of your money in your pocket. That's the core principle we're emphasizing here.

INVESTMENTS

Saving is crucial, but saving alone won't necessarily make you more comfortable with your 40-hour-a-week job, especially without overtime. In fact, with the right investments, you might not even need to work a full 40 hours and could potentially retire early. But let's not get too far ahead of ourselves; let's start with the basics of investing. Keep in mind that what works for one person might not work for another, so it's essential to find an approach that suits you and can benefit you the most.

One of the primary forms of investing is the stock market. I understand that investing in stocks can seem daunting, with questions like, "Where do I start?" or "What if I lose money?" or "Where should I invest my money?" In 2023, there are numerous resources available to help beginners learn about trading. I remember reading "A Random Walk Down Wall Street," which helped me grasp the concepts of index and ETF trading, allowing me to grow my investments passively in what we refer to as "safe stocks." There is a plethora of beginner-friendly books on trading, and if that's overwhelming, I've given you one recommendation. If that's not sufficient, consider seeking guidance from a professional or someone close to you with experience in stock market investing. If I don't emphasize anything else, please remember that thorough research is crucial before you commit your money. Without proper knowledge, you could be throwing your hard-earned savings into the abyss. Even if it takes months before you make your first investment, it's okay, as long as you're taking the first step into investing and not squandering your savings by jumping into the stock market blindly. Take your time and research thoroughly before you start trading.

Trading isn't the sole way to invest or generate passive income. Many people overlook the Certificate of Deposit (CD) account. This account allows you to deposit a specific amount of money with a fixed annual percentage that you earn on top of your deposit each year or every few months, depending on the bank, the time of year, and the market. It's a suitable option for those who want to earn interest on their money without the risks of the stock market. For instance, if you have $500 in a CD account for 5 years at 4.00%, you will earn around $108 in guaranteed money. It may not seem like a significant amount, but your money is growing steadily and securely. This is one of the most passive ways to watch your money grow without any active involvement. Most major banks offer CD options, but the annual percentages can vary, so it's essential to research and find the best fit for your needs. CD terms can range from as short as 6 months to as long as 10 years.

When discussing savings, I can't forget to mention high-yield savings accounts. Unlike a CD, you can withdraw money from a high-yield savings account as needed without facing penalties. If you're unsure whether you might need access to your savings for emergencies, bills, or other unforeseen circumstances, this type of account is a suitable choice. You can grow your money while maintaining access to it. Ultimately, choose what aligns with your financial goals, but remember that saving in any form is beneficial, and making your money grow is always a positive step. Reach out to your local banks to find the best savings account deals that offer compound interest on your initial deposit.

Now, if you're looking for something less risky with the potential for higher rewards, you can consider investing in bonds, specifically government bonds. If you're unfamiliar with what a bond is, it's essentially a loan from an investor (you) to a borrower, which could be the government or a corporation. You might be wondering why you should do this. Well, similar to a Certificate of Deposit (CD) or a savings account, the goal is to make more money without actively working for it.

Government bonds have some distinct characteristics. Many of them come with a fixed 30-year period, unlike shorter-term options like 5-month or 10-year bonds. If you decide to invest in government bonds, make sure you don't need the money you're putting away. Think of it like throwing a boomerang; it'll come back to you when you least expect it. Attempting to withdraw it early can result in penalties, and these penalties can be higher than those associated with a CD account. Keep in mind that the compound interest on government bonds can be higher than both a CD and a savings account, so consider this when making your decision. Your money is protected and backed by the government with any of these accounts; it's just a matter of determining how long you can afford to let your money sit.

I mentioned corporate bonds briefly, but let's delve deeper into them so you can understand the key differences between government bonds and corporate bonds. Corporate bonds work similarly to government bonds, but one of the key distinctions is that you're making a deal with a company rather than the government. This means it's a riskier loan, but higher risk can lead to higher rewards. However, I want to emphasize that when dealing with loans of this kind, if you're not prepared to invest money you don't need in the near future or can't afford to lose, it might not be the right choice for you.

In other words, with corporate bonds, if you anticipate needing the money soon or can't take the risk of losing it, you should probably steer clear. Another important point to note is that if the yield of the bond is higher, there's a chance that the business really needs the loan or might be facing financial difficulties. Typically, larger companies offer lower yields for their bonds.

I can't discuss investing without mentioning one of the biggest markets out there, which is real estate. I know you've probably heard this a thousand times, but it can definitely help you generate passive income. However, similar to compound interest, you'll need more than one piece of real estate to start making substantial money. I won't sit here and claim that it's easy or that you can buy your first house with no money down. What I can tell you is that a good credit score can help you secure a lower interest rate on the loan you'll need for your new home. There are numerous programs to assist first-time homebuyers, such as the FHA loan, a government-backed option that offers some of the lowest interest rates on the market to help you become a homeowner.

Now, I understand you might be thinking, "Owning a home is expensive," and you're absolutely right. However, it doesn't have to be a financial burden. You can use your first home as a rental property, with tenants covering your mortgage, allowing you to collect income each month. But before you jump in, remember that it's not as easy as it sounds; thorough research is crucial. I'll emphasize this repeatedly throughout this book: Research, Research, Research. This is the most important step before you invest your hard-earned money anywhere other than your own pocket. The goal is to preserve as much of your money as possible while also growing it, not risking it like a gamble. You shouldn't treat money like you're in a casino; make sure you fully understand what you're investing in.

Another point worth mentioning is that there are various types of real estate, including commercial, corporate, housing, residential, and more. There's a type of real estate for almost any purpose, even land. All of these can potentially generate income, whether on a large or small scale. Increasing your wealth at any level is beneficial for you and your family. Remember when I talked about good debt? Real estate is one of the best ways to incur good debt, as it can generate more income than you put into it.

However, a word of caution: always maintain savings and never invest your last dime in property. If something goes wrong, you need to have the means to address it, and you certainly don't want to find yourself in a deeper financial hole. That could leave you trapped in a never-ending cycle of working solely to pay off the loan you took out. The loan that was originally meant for good debt can turn into a burden if not managed carefully. This is something you should avoid at all costs, so refrain from investing your last resources into property, especially if you haven't thoroughly researched the market or the specific property you're interested in.

A book that was incredibly helpful to me and could benefit you as well is "Rich Dad, Poor Dad" by Robert T. Kiyosaki. It's an excellent resource for understanding the basics of real estate investing. Remember, there are countless different ways to invest your money; you just have to find what works best for you.

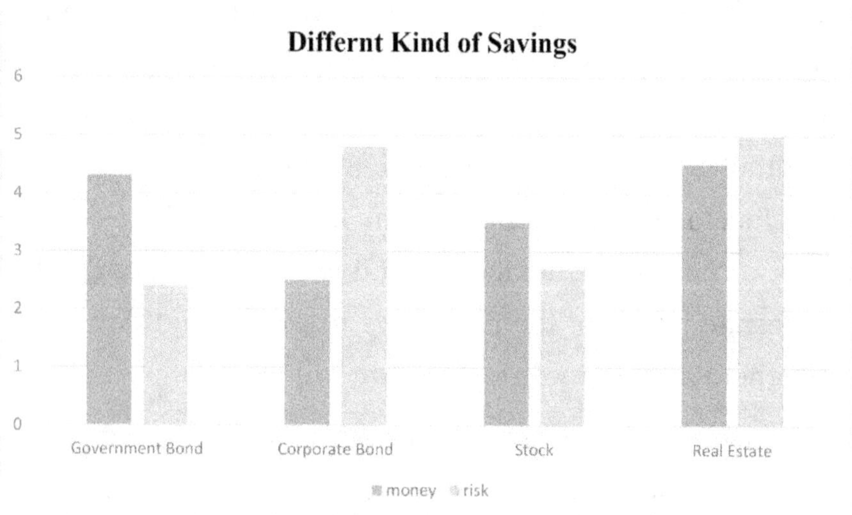

In the chart above, it displays the possible risks and rewards of various types of investments. Select the one that aligns better with your preferences.

Which method do you believe is the most favorable, and what is your reasoning behind this choice?

____

____

____

BUDGETING

Daily	Home	Work	Other
Monday			
Tuesday			
Wednesday			
Thursday			
Friday			
Saturday			
Sunday			

One of the most crucial aspects, which you probably already know (but if you don't, it's time to learn), is budgeting. Budgeting serves a dual purpose, benefiting both your future planning and your daily planning. In the chart above, I'd like you to take a seat and start calculating a few things for me. First, calculate how much money you spend on a daily basis. This is what they refer to as day-to-day spending in the business world.

Afterward, I want you to set aside an amount representing how much money you could save by reducing this type of expenditure. This approach will help you cut down on unnecessary spending and eliminate those extra expenses.

WEEKLY SPENDING

Per week	Home	Work	Other
Week 1			
Week 2			
Week 3			
Week 4			

This time, I'd like you to assess your weekly spending, not on a daily basis but by calculating the total expenditure for each week throughout the month. You can achieve this by reviewing your old bank statements and adding up all the expenses, excluding your bills. I want you to focus more on items that you don't absolutely need, such as those Target trips – you know, the ones where you go in for one thing and come out with much more than you initially intended. This also encompasses online shopping.

Before you begin, understand that this exercise is meant to help you realize how much money you've been spending on things that aren't essential. Once you've done that, compile the data and see how much unnecessary money you've spent by the end of the month.

Months	Home	Work	Other
Jan			
Feb			
March			
April			
May			
June			
July			
August			
September			
October			
November			
December			

Now, I want you to repeat the same process, but this time, do it month by month. When you're done, add up how much you typically spend in a year on non-essential items. After that, carefully review your list item by item to identify areas where you can cut down. Keep in mind that we're not including essential bills because those are necessary for shelter and to create a surplus of extra cash.

Once you've completed this exercise, make a list of how much extra money you would have after paying all your bills and allocating most of it to savings and/or investments. Remember that results won't happen overnight; it might take months to see significant changes depending on your spending habits and what you consider an expense.

Keep in mind that what one person considers an expense, another might not. Do what's best for you, and don't leave anything out. This exercise is meant to help you save and reduce unnecessary costs. If you're committed to improvement, don't shy away from it.

Now, let me ask you, what extra expenses do you plan on cutting, and which ones will you keep?

____

____

____

____

____

____

____

____

____

BAD DEBT

We discussed what good debt is; now, let's take a look at the other side because there are always two sides to every coin. Bad debt, by definition, is simply debt that you can't repay. However, that's not necessarily what bad debt entails. Let me provide you with an example. Many people might consider taking out a loan as bad debt, but it often depends on the purpose of that loan. If you've borrowed money for a business venture that will generate income in a few months or a couple of years, I would consider that good debt, as you're planning to make money from it.

On the other hand, bad debt, in my view, is when you take out a loan solely to pay your bills, and you receive nothing in return. You're essentially giving away money instead of using it to generate more significant returns. Another example of bad debt is credit cards. With credit cards, you not only have to repay the money but also face a high Annual Percentage Rate (APR), like 15% or 20%. So, in addition to repaying the principal amount, you're also paying interest on each purchase. This doesn't seem like a favorable deal, which is why people often caution against using credit cards for this reason. Furthermore, if you don't pay your credit card balance on time, you'll be charged the APR plus late fees, pushing you deeper into debt, making it increasingly challenging to escape.

A valuable rule of thumb I've learned when dealing with credit cards, which nobody told me about, is that if you don't have the cash readily available to pay off the credit card balance, then you shouldn't make the purchase. This practice will save you from headaches and unnecessary debt. The goal here is to get out of debt, not to accumulate more.

I mentioned loans earlier, and some can be either good or bad, depending on their purpose. One of the worst financial moves you can make is taking out a loan to pay off another loan. Yes, you read that correctly. In doing so, you're merely shifting your debt from one creditor to another. However, there is an exception to this rule; only consider it if your current loan has an exceptionally high APR, and the new loan offers a lower one. In this case, you'll still be in debt, but you'll have to pay slightly less interest to the new creditor. Nevertheless, I strongly advise against taking out a loan unless you genuinely need it or it will help you generate income.

This decision could have long-term financial repercussions, even if you don't see them right away. It could negatively impact your credit score, which typically takes seven years to recover from if you're unable to repay the loan you've taken out.

<u>Now, let's consider student loans. Do you think they fall under the category of good credit or bad? And why?</u>

____

____

____

____

____

____

____

____

____

____

To answer the question, student loans fall under the category of good debt, and I'll explain why. When you take out a student loan, you're investing in your education and future. Most people take out these loans with the goal of increasing their earning potential, not diminishing it. For example, when aspiring to become a doctor or lawyer, you're willing to take out a loan to pursue your education, pass exams, and eventually practice your profession, which will enable you to pay back the loans and maintain a comfortable lifestyle. So, remember this as you embark on your educational journey or consider taking out a loan for education: the aim is to acquire knowledge and skills that will lead to a more prosperous future.

Now, let's discuss automobile debt. While many people require cars, especially if they live outside urban areas, it doesn't mean you should stretch your finances to the breaking point to afford one. It's unnecessary to drive an expensive foreign car that, when it breaks down, you can't even afford to repair, leaving you with a car loan and a non-functional vehicle. This doesn't sound like a wise choice, does it? If you need a car, aim for one that's reasonably priced and doesn't have to be a foreign luxury car. What you truly need is a reliable vehicle that won't strain your finances. Consider this: would you prefer a car that gets you to work reliably and allows you to afford any necessary repairs, or would you rather buy something well beyond your financial means, and when issues arise, it pushes you further into financial hardship? Whatever you decide, make smart financial choices and avoid accumulating bad debt simply to maintain an image, because when things go wrong, you're the one left with the responsibility of paying it back, no one else. Additionally, keep in mind that cars lose value as soon as you drive them off the lot, meaning you won't recoup the full price even if you sell it. This underscores the importance of repaying that loan, even if you decide to sell the vehicle.

GOOD DEBT	BAD DEBT
Buying a House	Automobile
Student Loans	Credit Card
Business loan	Payday loans

HOW?

This is the million-dollar question, isn't it? I've discussed some ways you can save money, but now, let's talk about why you might find it challenging to save money. There could be a million reasons why saving money seems difficult, but are we here to make excuses? Even though a significant portion of the responsibility lies with you, such as spending rapidly, being unable to say no, or attempting to maintain a lifestyle beyond your budget, there are also external factors that hinder people from saving.

One common complaint, even from my own experience, is the rapid rate of inflation. Worldwide, the prices of basic necessities are rising, including food, gas, and even water bills. Yes, even water bills keep increasing at a rapid pace. This means that even if you cut out certain activities and eat at home, you might still struggle to save because everything else has become so expensive. Not only is inflation on the rise, but jobs aren't providing sufficient raises to keep up with it, and rent prices are skyrocketing more than ever before. The economy has many complex factors that make saving quite challenging. In fact, this year, people are saving much less on average compared to last year. So, if you're finding it tough to start saving, don't feel disheartened. Even if you begin slowly, you'll still be ahead of many others. According to Yahoo, about 10% of people have only $1,000 in their savings account.

Don't let this information make you afraid to save money or think that you'll never escape your current debt. Where there's a will, there's a way, no matter what. There are always solutions, especially when it comes to saving and getting out of debt. The economy may not be in the best shape, but that doesn't mean you have to become a victim of it. Also, keep in mind that if you're reading this book, you're likely above average in financial awareness, so these statistics might not apply to you if you follow the methods you've found and will continue to find throughout this book to save more and spend less.

One crucial thing to remember is that no matter the financial challenges you're facing, they could be much worse. But before things take a turn for the worse, we're going to try to prevent that by taking many steps. There's always a plan to get out of debt; you just have to follow through with it and stop procrastinating.

<u>So, what's stopping you from saving money? And why?</u>

MONEY

Money, what is it? Well, money is a piece of paper or digital currency used to acquire the things you want or need to live and survive. We've discussed how to save money and how to increase your wealth, but we haven't delved into how money directly impacts you. Understanding how something can affect you, whether positively or negatively, is crucial. Research has shown that a lack of money or constant worry about finances can lead to depression, unlike those who are financially secure.

Financial well-being has a direct correlation with physical health, much like the effects of stress. Both can leave you in poor physical condition. Like many people, if you don't have enough money for basic necessities, it can dominate your thoughts day and night, and I, myself, have experienced this. It can disrupt your sleep, cause frustration, hinder your willingness to engage in activities due to financial constraints, and sometimes even lead to irritability or outright anger. While not everyone experiences these emotions, they are common because money plays a pivotal role in our lives, and without it, our world can come to a halt.

You might be unable to pay rent, provide for yourself, access basic needs like food, afford a gym membership, or even access necessary medical care due to its steep cost. These are all factors that can impact both your mental and physical health.

<u>What else can a lack of money affect in your life?</u>

The basic necessities of life require money, such as food, shelter, clothing, and sleep. According to psychology, without these basic needs, you will find yourself miserable. Consider this: these are the fundamental requirements for living, and all of them necessitate some form of income. Once you have your financial aspect in order and enough resources, you can begin to experience greater happiness, as you won't lie awake at night worrying about how to feed yourself or pay your rent. If you have children or a family to provide for, the pressure intensifies because you're not only concerned about yourself but also about the well-being of others. Many people depend on you and your income, making it even more crucial.

I've spoken to many individuals who have shared their concerns about not being financially stable and how it has affected their emotional well-being, often leading to depression. So, before you spend money on frequenting clubs, bars, or going out every week, ask yourself if you have enough to cover life's necessities. And if you do, reconsider if you have three times the amount needed before indulging. Remember, you want to live comfortably, not just barely keeping your head above water. This is vital to remember because every weekend, when you're about to head out, I want you to reflect on this and question whether spending money on wants rather than needs is the right choice.

Once you've crossed the first stage and have secured the money you need for your basic needs, shift your focus to the next stage, which is security or safety needs. This level is about taking care of your health because once financial worries are alleviated, you can truly start taking care of yourself. This includes exercising regularly and maintaining a healthy diet. Additionally, it's important to mention job security to ensure a steady income, although I understand that in today's economy, this can be challenging. Nonetheless, strive to achieve it, and once all these pieces are in place, we can move on to the next stage.

This stage is equally significant because you'll feel better with everything covered, and you'll be ready to rejoin the world, build friendships, relationships, and connections. This is possible because you're no longer struggling and constantly worrying about the next paycheck. A side note: you don't always have to spend money to have fun with your loved ones, and if you always have to spend money when you're with them, are they truly your loved ones? This includes friends, family, and romantic partners.

In my view, this is the most crucial stage, although it may not be the same for everyone. It's essential to notice the pattern of increasing happiness as we ascend this pyramid. As humans, we are social creatures, which is why socializing holds such importance higher up in the hierarchy. The simple answer is that you have to take care of yourself first; you come before anyone else. If you're not okay, how can you ensure that everyone else is? With that clarified, this stage is about self-esteem. The reason I suggest it should be lower on the list or even the first step is that without self-esteem, you may find it difficult to achieve many things if you're constantly doubting yourself. At least that's how it applies to me. It may vary for you, but when you possess self-esteem and believe in yourself, you can conquer anything in the world, from finding a new job to discovering new resources. Believing in yourself leads to confidence, which can open numerous doors and help you overcome depression caused by financial constraints.

The last and final step in what I call basic happiness is self-actualization. If you're not familiar with the term, it means realizing your potential and striving to become the best version of yourself possible. This entails consistent self-improvement, whether it's in terms of physical health, aiming for the highest job promotion, or seeking a better partner than your ex. This step is last for a reason because at this point, nothing should be holding you back, as you've mastered the previous four stages. Your mind is clear, you're doing your best, and life is good. However, it's important to remember that you can't skip the first four steps in the process to reach this stage. Life is a journey, and this is a crucial part of it.

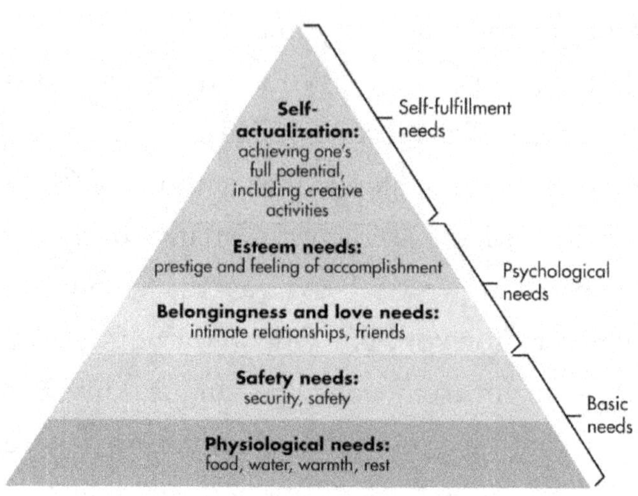

<u>Which level of Maslow pyramid are you? And what would help you get to the next level?</u>

____

____

____

____

____

____

____

WE ARE NOT DONE

We've discussed some ways to save, but now let's dive deeper and explore even more advanced methods to save your money. One crucial aspect that often goes unnoticed is the indirect marketing that influences our buying decisions. A prime example of this is the emails we receive, such as those from Fashion Nova or Walmart, enticing us with offers to save big. These emails subtly encourage you to make purchases, often without you even realizing it, similar to how you may talk about something and then see an advertisement for it on social media.

The first step you should take is to unsubscribe from emails that tempt you to buy things you may not actually need. Remember, anything beyond your basic necessities falls into the category of "wants," and for now, you need to cut down on your "wants" to achieve your financial goals.

One of the most underrated strategies in today's society is buying used items instead of new ones. If you desire something but also want to save money, consider searching for it in a used condition, whether it's a phone, tablet, car, or any other item. Especially in an era where new versions of phones and tablets are released annually with minor upgrades, the difference between new and used may not be significant. The money saved by buying used can be redirected towards investments that will help you grow your wealth instead of simply spending it.

Here's an old-school favorite of mine that has worked well for me and can hopefully work well for you too. I put money in an envelope and set it aside until the next payday, adding more to it each time. This serves both as emergency funding and a way to prevent me from spending my entire paycheck within the pay period. After paying bills and setting aside my regular savings, I allocate a small portion just before the next payday to this envelope. It demonstrates my discipline in not living paycheck to paycheck and highlights the various ways I can save and allocate my money, rather than keeping it all in a bank. You can give this a try; even small contributions count. Do it throughout the year, and when you open the envelope at the end of the year, you'll be surprised at how much you've saved, all while ensuring you've paid your bills, contributed to your regular savings, and made investments.

Are you holding onto items you no longer use or wear? If you're not a hoarder, then why not sell those items? You can make a decent amount of money by selling unused or unworn items, and it's incredibly convenient to sell things online without the need for a physical garage sale. Why not make money while you're making money? There's no point in keeping items around the house that serve no purpose, so start selling. People often overlook the little things that can help them save or make money, but even the smallest efforts can add up.

This may seem obvious, but it's worth mentioning: cancel subscriptions that you no longer need or use. This can save you money. If you have cable, consider whether you truly need it or if different streaming subscriptions would be more beneficial, given that every network seems to offer its own subscription service these days. Choose the one that suits you best instead of juggling multiple subscriptions. Additionally, if you've been with a company for a while, don't hesitate to ask for a raise. If your current employer is unwilling to provide one, explore opportunities in the same field that offer higher pay and consider applying there. A raise can significantly contribute to your financial goals.

Changing your choice of supermarket can also make a difference, as some are more budget-friendly than others. It might be slightly out of your way, but the savings on groceries each week can accumulate over the month or year. You can then reinvest those savings to further your financial growth. The ultimate goal is to make your money grow by spending less, saving more, and investing wisely. There are countless ways to save; you just need to be willing to seek them out and learn how to implement them effectively.

WHAT MANY PEOPLE DON'T KNOW

We've discussed many topics thus far, but one thing we haven't touched upon is credit. What exactly is credit, why is it crucial for us to maintain good credit, and how can we achieve that?

<u>Tell me, what is your understanding of credit and your credit score?</u>

For those who may not be familiar with the concept of credit, it essentially involves a contractual agreement where a borrower receives a sum of money or some other valuable item and commits to repaying the lender at a later date, often with added interest. In simpler terms, it means borrowing money from someone else and agreeing to pay it back. For instance, if you borrow money from a friend to cover bills or grab a meal, with the promise to pay them back on your next payday or when you have some extra cash, you're essentially borrowing on credit. In this scenario, your friend is extending a loan to you on credit since you currently lack the funds to cover the expense yourself. The more you borrow and successfully repay, the stronger your credit relationship becomes with that person or financial institution.

People often wonder how to establish good credit with banks or how to build their credit, and there are several ways to achieve this goal. Surprisingly, building credit is one of the easiest financial accomplishments. Numerous credit cards are available that can assist you in building your credit, but always remember the fundamental rule of credit building: consistently repay what you've spent on your credit card. This rule is paramount, and if you adhere to it, you can witness substantial progress in your credit score in a matter of months. The rate of progress depends on both your credit card expenditure and the promptness of your repayments.

Rule number two: strive not to spend more than 30% of your credit limit. If your credit limit is $100, avoid exceeding $30 in charges, or at least make a conscious effort not to. This demonstrates that you're not overly reliant on your credit card for all your expenses. Rule number three advises making multiple payments, including the monthly minimum and any additional payments you can afford, to pay off your card more rapidly. Keep in mind that you can create your own set of rules, but the ones I've outlined have helped me maintain an excellent credit score.

Nevertheless, it's crucial to understand that various factors come into play when determining how your credit score is affected. One key consideration is the length of time you've held a particular credit card, as this is also taken into account. Additionally, the number of active credit cards you possess influences your credit score. When you apply for a new credit card, the credit bureau takes notice, and it can impact your credit score as well. While there is an abundance of credit card options available, choose wisely, as your choice can also affect your credit. Don't be intimidated by these factors; as long as you follow the rules I've provided, your credit score can steadily improve over time, as long as you consistently make on-time payments.

Missing payments on your credit card or loans can have a significantly negative impact on your credit score, potentially lasting up to seven years. This is the duration for which a negative mark on your credit score can linger. Therefore, it is of utmost importance to prevent such situations and make every effort to avoid late or missed payments. While unforeseen circumstances such as job loss or financial difficulties can arise, making every possible effort to meet your payment obligations is crucial. Late or missed payments can affect the interest rates you receive on future loans or financial commitments, whether you're seeking a new credit card, applying for a loan to cover bills, or even purchasing a new car or home. Your credit score is the critical factor in these situations, so it's in your best interest to maintain it at the highest level possible.

The three major credit bureaus are Equifax, Experian, and Transunion. Together, these three companies determine your credit score and influence the interest rates you can secure on loans. If you're unsure about the quality of your credit score, you can always check it online at AnnualCreditReport.com. By law, they are obligated to provide you with your credit score from all three bureaus for free. You don't need to pay anything to access this information.

These credit bureaus provide details about your financial history, including the number of loans you've taken out, the length of your credit history, your outstanding debt, any late payments, the number of credit cards you've opened, and your monthly credit card payments. Additionally, they report if you've had any bankruptcies within the last 7-10 years or if you have a mortgage on a house. You can find all the information you need about your credit on that website. There's no need to rely on someone else to check your credit score when you can easily do it yourself.

Before opening your first or fifth credit card account, it's essential to be aware of various credit card types to make an informed decision. One credit card type I personally recommend is the rewards credit card, which allows you to earn rewards on all your purchases. However, remember that it's crucial to research different rewards cards, as some may offer better rewards than others.

The second type of credit card worth knowing about is the cashback credit card. This can be helpful when you need quick access to cash and don't have sufficient funds in your checking account. Similar to rewards cards, you earn money instead of rewards.

The third type is the secured credit card, which I consider the most responsible option. With a secured credit card, you deposit money to establish your credit line, effectively borrowing from yourself. This is an excellent way to build credit, especially if you have no credit history or credit cards.

For college students, a student credit card can be valuable as it can teach them about managing their finances and building credit from a young age. There are numerous credit card options available, but these are some important ones I believe are beneficial for the average person.

It's important to note that credit-building doesn't have to start at 18. Parents can add their children as authorized users on their credit cards, helping them start building their credit as soon as they turn 18. This head start can be a valuable gift for their future financial well-being.

CREDIT CARDS

Credit building	Intro APR	Purchase APR	Annual fee
Credit One Bank Platinum Visa for Rebuilding Credit	N/A	28.99%	$75 First year & $99 After
Capital One Quicksilver One Cash Rewards Credit Card	N/A	30.49%	$39
Milestone Mastercard	N/A	24.90%	$75 First year & $99 After
Avant Card	N/A	31.24%	$39
Indigo Mastercard	N/A	24.90%	$75 First year & $99 After
Citi Double Cash Card	N/A	19.24%-29.24%	$0

Upgrade Cash Rewards Visa	N/A	14.99%-29.99%	$0
Prosper Card	N/A	24.24%-35.24%	$0 With auto pay & $39 after first year.

These are just a few examples of credit cards that can assist you in building your credit, whether you have no credit history or a poor credit score. They can still be beneficial for your credit-building journey. Some cards are more favorable than others, but it's essential to conduct your research to determine which one aligns with your needs. Different options cater to different individuals.

Always keep in mind that there will be various choices available to you. Even if you've made mistakes with your credit in the past, there's always a path to rebuild and improve your credit score

NEVER GIVE UP

Everything might seem really tough at the beginning, but the more you practice, the easier it should become. Saving money shouldn't be something you dread or view as an overwhelming task. Regardless of where you start, whether it's a small amount or a large one, saving even a bit is better than saving nothing. Also, remember to do what works best for you. What may work for you might not work for others. Throughout this book, you will learn various methods for saving money, and even if not all of them work for you, you will find one that suits you best and stick to it. Eventually, you will reach your financial goal, whether it's in a month or perhaps even a year, even if it takes longer than you initially anticipated.

While you are saving, you can also work on building your credit at the same time. I like to call it "killing two birds with one stone." This approach will help you get ahead, even if you feel you're far behind. You don't have to rush to pay off all your loans and debt; as long as you don't miss payments and occasionally make extra payments, your credit should improve every month or every few months, depending on how often you check your credit. There are numerous ways to repair your credit, so never think that having a lot of debt means you can't also work on your credit and savings simultaneously. It all depends on how you manage the money you receive and the frequency of those inflows. Don't ever believe there's no solution to a problem, as there's always a way to fix things. You just have to think outside the box and explore new avenues.

There's one more crucial thing you should be aware of: if you choose to go into default on your credit cards or loans, it will remain on your credit report for up to 7 years, marked as a hard inquiry. This could significantly impact your credit score and affect the APR you'll receive on future loans, which tend to be higher. Moreover, you may struggle to secure a loan during that 7-year period. That's why I always advise against going into default unless it's an absolute last resort. If you think 7 years isn't a long time, just remember that it's roughly the duration from junior high to college – a substantial portion of your life. So, keep that in mind if you're contemplating such a decision. If you absolutely must go down that path and have no other choice, remember the consequences, including non-stop calls from debt collectors trying to collect the money from you. One more thing to remember is that if your debt goes into default and someone other than the original borrower contacts you to repay the debt, do not engage, as they are not the party you had an agreement with. However, I strongly recommend avoiding this situation altogether and making an effort to pay off your debts without letting them accumulate or go into default.

LINK TO SOURCES

https://www.businessinsider.com/personal-finance/average-american-debt

https://www.forbes.com/sites/forbesfinancecouncil/2018/10/25/what-percentage-of-small-businesses-fail-and-how-can-you-avoid-being-one-of-them/?sh=2475d47943b5

https://www.uc.edu/news/articles/2023/04/americans-spend-more-at-restaurants-than-on-groceries.html#:~:text=Americans%20spent%20more%20money%20at,Cincinnati%20economist%20told%20Spectrum%20News.&text=According%20to%20the%20U.S.%20Census,than%20on%20groceries%20last%20year.

https://www.stocktrader.com/best-stock-trading-books

https://www.cnbc.com/select/what-is-an-fha-loan/

https://www.investopedia.com/terms/r/realestate.asp

https://www.debt.org/advice/good-vs-bad/

https://www.simplypsychology.org/maslow.html#:~:text=There%20are%20five%20levels%20in,esteem%2C%20and%20self%2Dactualization.

https://www.bankrate.com/finance/credit-cards/different-types-of-credit-cards/#secured

https://www.creditkarma.com/credit-cards/fair-credit?adcampaign=Credit_Cards_revmar_ggl-search_all-web_none_general_exact&adcopy=14832392320_1463994532 31_635008941004&adgroup=cc-fair

ABOUT AUTHOR

Courtland Thompson, a self-help author, draws from a working class background in psychology, sociology and personal development. With a bachelor's degree in communication and a decade of experience as a life coach, Courtland has empowered countless individuals to navigate life's challenges. His writing seamlessly combines research-backed strategies with personal Strategies, creating a transformative experience for readers seeking growth and fulfillment. As a dedicated advocate for financial growth, and personal development Courtland mission is to inspire positive change and guide readers on their journey to a more resilient and empowered life.